Why do camels have humps?

Disney BOOKS BY MAIL

When Mickey Wonders Why, he searches out
the answers with a little
help from these friendly experts:

DK Direct Limited
Managing Art Editor Eljay Crompton
Senior Editor Rosemary McCormick
Writer Alexandra Parsons
Illustrators The Alvin White Studios and Richard Manning
Designers Wayne Blades, Veneta Bullen, Richard Clemson,
Sarah Goodwin, Diane Klein, Sonia Whillock

Contents

Why do woodpeckers peck trees?

To find food. Woodpeckers eat little insect grubs, beetles, and ants that live in or under the bark of trees. They pick up the insects with their very long, very sticky tongues before they have time to run away!

Home sweet home
You guessed it! Most woodpeckers make their homes by drilling holes in trees!

Headache? No siree!
You'd think the poor old woodpecker would get one mighty big headache from all that pecking, but it doesn't. Its skull and beak are specially designed to prevent headaches.

Tap, tap, peck!

Woodpeckers may peck up to 12,000 times a day.

The European green woodpecker will gobble up thousands of ants in just one day.

The acorn woodpecker drills holes in trees to store its winter food supply of hundreds of acorns.

Why do birds fly south in winter?

To find food and warmer weather. But they don't just fly south, they fly north, too. That's because when it's summer in one part of the world, it's winter in another. So the birds that fly south have laid their eggs and brought up their baby chicks during the northern summer months, and as winter approaches, they fly south to warmer weather.

Bye, bye
Why do some birds fly south in winter?
Because it's too far to walk!

A long swim
Birds aren't the only ones that travel. Young eels that grow up in Europe and North America swim all the way to the Sargasso Sea in the Caribbean to lay their eggs.

A long flight
The Arctic tern is a long-distance traveler. When summer ends it leaves the Arctic and flies 11,000 miles to Antarctica. At the end of the Antarctic summer it flies back to the Arctic. That adds up to 22,000 miles!

Travelers' tales

☞ Birds that fly to warmer places are called migratory birds.

☞ Geese have been seen flying over the Himalayas at almost 30,000 feet! That's as tall as 24 empire state buildings.

hy do camels have humps?

So they always have some stored-up energy, just in case they don't get anything to eat or drink for months. Camels' humps are lumps of stored fat. When there is no food to eat, or water to drink, camels use their fat store. Because of this, camels can live in the desert where there are only a few prickly bushes.

8

One hump or two?
If a camel has two humps, like this one, it is a bactrian camel from the deserts of Asia. If it has one hump, it is an African or Arabian camel, called a dromedary.

Useful friends

☞ Both camels and llamas can carry heavy loads, and walk for miles and miles. But camels can do something llamas can't – they can go for eight or nine months without a drink of water!

Tasty shakes
What do you get if you cross a cow with a camel?
Lumpy milkshakes.

Relation with no humps
Llamas come from South America. Although they don't have humps, they are related to the camel. They live in mountain areas where it is very cold at night, so llamas have thick, shaggy coats to keep them warm.

What is a manatee?

Even though it looks like a seal, or sea lion, it's really an underwater cow. The manatee is a mammal that lives in the water and grazes on water grasses and weeds. (Mammals are warm-blooded animals that feed their young with milk.) They are peaceful, quiet, and friendly animals.

All together now!
Manatees play together and often kiss each other when they meet. They seldom come out of the water, but if they do, they wriggle their way back again.

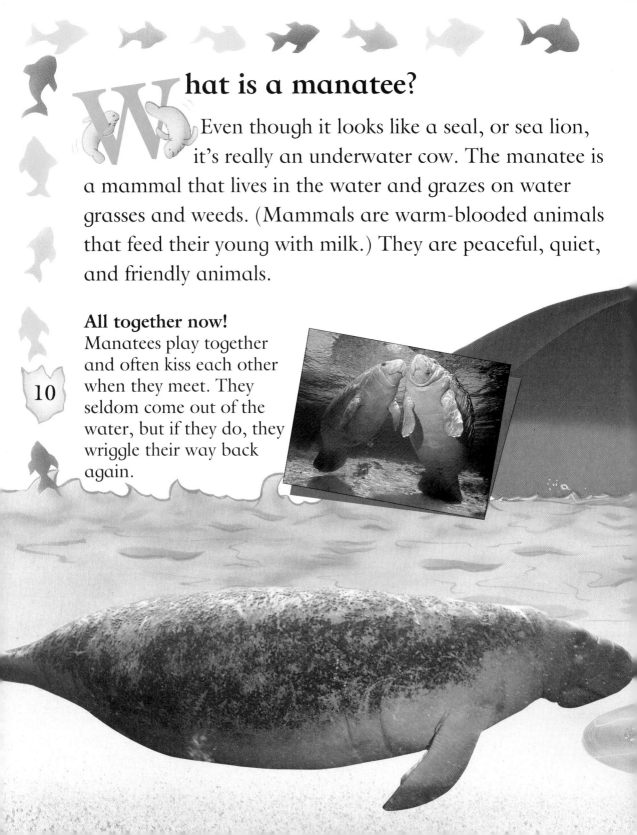

Cute baby

Baby manatees are born under water. Then they are helped to the surface by their mothers, to breathe for the first time.

Manatee facts

☞ Manatees don't see very well. They often bump into things in the water. Whoops!

☞ Manatees can stay under water for up to 15 minutes without coming up for air.

☞ Manatees use their tails as paddles and sometimes "walk" along under water on their flippers.

11

ow do otters eat their dinner?

They float on their backs. Otters use their chests as tables, and flat stones to break open the shells of the seafood they love to eat. When they have finished their meal, they just turn over so the crumbs are washed away. Isn't that a great way to do the dishes!

Sweet dreams!
Otters spend most of their time in the water. They even sleep in the water. They lie on their backs and sometimes place their paws over their eyes. Sea otters also wrap themselves in seaweed attached to the ocean floor to make sure they don't drift away.

Wheeeee!

River otters like to play games. They especially love to slide down muddy banks into the river.

Otter facts

☞ Otters can swim at 10 mph – which is about as fast as you can run.

☞ Otters eat fish, shellfish, birds, frogs, and insects.

☞ Unlike most water animals, otters don't have a layer of fat under their skin for warmth.

13

Why is the duck-billed platypus so mixed up?

Because it acts, and looks like, many different animals all rolled into one. The duck-billed platypus (PLAT-i-pus) lays eggs, just like birds and reptiles do. But it feeds its babies on milk, just like mammals do. And, to make things even more confusing, it also has webbed feet and a beak just like a duck.

River home!
Platypus families live in riverside burrows. The burrows have long, curved tunnels to confuse their enemies.

14

Platypus feet facts

 The platypus has feet like no other animal. Its front feet are webbed, just like ducks' feet, to help it swim. But the web part folds back like an umbrella. So when it wants to use its feet for digging, it can.

Little babies
These are baby duck-billed platypuses. The mommy lays the eggs and waits about 10 days for them to hatch.

Why do skunks smell?

They don't. But skunks can make others smell if they sense danger. Then they raise their tail and squirt out a horrible-smelling liquid. One whiff of this stuff is so bad that a skunk's enemy will soon run away.

Danger signs!
In the animal world, stripes and spots mean something. The yellow and black stripes on this deadly poisonous toad mean – DANGER! I'M POISONOUS! I COULD BE YOUR LAST MEAL!

16

Smelly facts

☞ The little spotted skunk puts on a great show to keep enemies away. First it stamps its front feet and sticks up its tail. If that doesn't do the trick, it does a handstand. But if that doesn't work – it's smelly time!

Skunk alert!
How do you stop a skunk from smelling?
Hold its nose.

Hold your nose!
The skunk has a gland under its tail which makes the smelly liquid. It can spray from as far as 12 feet, AND hit its target!

Why don't chickens fly?

Because they have short, rounded wings that aren't made for flying. All they can do is flutter up onto a low branch if they need to. So chickens spend their time on the ground, running here and there on their strong legs and pecking around the farmyard.

The first chicken
All chickens are related in some way to this handsome red jungle fowl.

Time to come out
It takes a baby chick exactly 21 days to grow inside its egg. When it is ready to meet Mom, it will peck its way out of the egg using a little bump on its beak called the egg tooth.

Chicken facts

👉 Female chickens are called hens.

👉 Male chickens are called roosters. They are the ones that cock-a-doodle-do loudly in the morning.

👉 Did you know that there's a chicken named after the state of Rhode Island?

Cluck, cluck!
Who tells chicken jokes?
Comedi-hens!

Why do squirrels store nuts?

So they will have something to eat in the chilly months when food is harder to find. In fall, squirrels bury little piles of nuts and seeds in holes in the ground. In winter, they scurry out of their cozy nests to munch on their winter supply. But sometimes, because the buried snacks are harder to sniff, the squirrels never find the food and it stays buried forever!

Squirrels' dessert
Squirrels sometimes
strip bark from trees
to get at the sweet
sap underneath.

Look out!
Believe it or not, this
is a flying squirrel.
It glides through
the air from
tree to tree.

Squirrel facts

Squirrels can tell good
nuts from bad nuts
without cracking them
open. They feel the weight
of them in their front
paws. A heavy nut is
usually a good nut, but a
light nut is probably all
dried up inside.

re bats really blind?

No, they are not. There are lots of different kinds of bats, and some of them can see better than others. (Bats are nocturnal animals. This means they sleep all day and wake up at night.) Fruit bats, for instance, can see pretty well in the dark, but insect-eating bats cannot see as well, and they rely on their hearing to get around.

Big ears

Bats have very sensitive ears and they can hear the echoes from the high-pitched squeaks they make. By figuring out how long an echo takes to bounce back, the bat knows how far away an object is.

More fruit please!

This fruit bat likes to eat fruit. No surprise, huh? A fruit bat has a mouth like a lemon squeezer. It uses its tongue to squash fruit against jagged ridges in the roof of its mouth.

Bat facts

☞ Bats have a very good sense of smell.

☞ Some bats spend their day in dark caves. Others sleep in hollow trees.

☞ Bats are the only mammals that can fly.

How can some animals see in the dark?

Because they have big eyes with pupils that can open wide. (The pupil is the black circle in the center of the eye that lets light in.) Their eyes are big so that they can collect all of the little light there is from the moon and the stars to help them see.

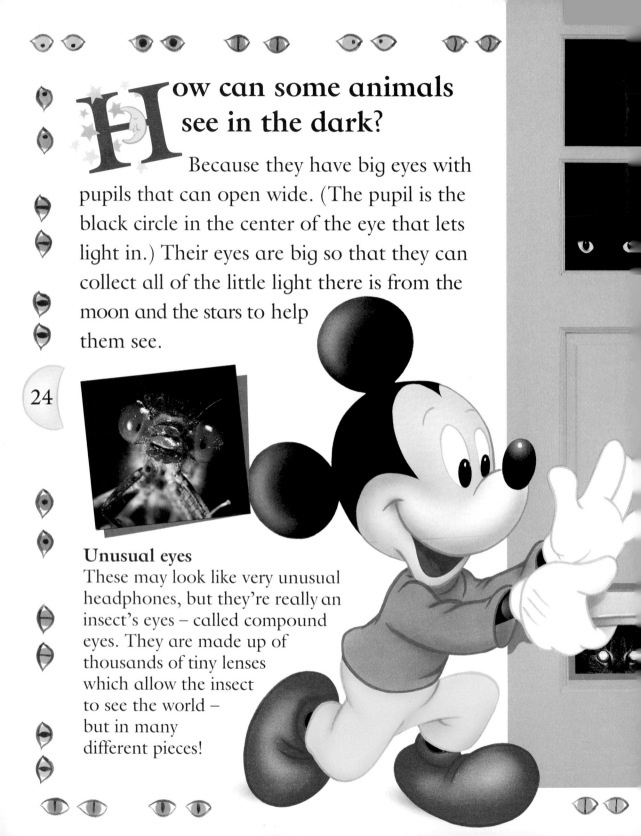

Unusual eyes
These may look like very unusual headphones, but they're really an insect's eyes – called compound eyes. They are made up of thousands of tiny lenses which allow the insect to see the world – but in many different pieces!

Mirror eyes

Animals that can see in the dark have a layer of tissue at the back of the eye that acts like a mirror. It bounces light back through the pupil – and that's what makes some nighttime animals' eyes shine in the dark.

The eyes have it

A snail's eyes are on the end of its antennae.

Other animals that see well at night are deer, bush babies and geckos.

Animals that come out at night usually can't see colors – except for cats!

Why do fireflies glow?

It's just their way of getting noticed! Fireflies have special chemicals in their bodies that glow with a bright light. When they want to say hello to each other, they flash their lights on and off like twinkling stars in the night sky.

All lit up!
These fireflies put on a spectacular show at nighttime. After a little practice, all the fireflies in one tree flash on and off in perfect harmony!

A special code
This is a female firefly. She is much bigger than the male. You can get a firefly to fly onto your finger if you can copy its flashes with a flashlight.

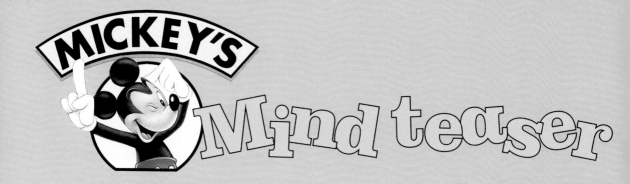

Can you remember why these animals don't need these items?

Shed some light on it!

☞ Fireflies are not flies, but night-flying beetles.

☞ Just like an airplane, the female North American firefly keeps flashing her taillight until she lands.